The Best Air Fryer

Cookbook

Delicious Quick and Easy Air Fryer Recipes for
Diabetic People. Cut Cholesterol, Heal Your Body
and Regain Confidence to Start Live a Proper
Lifestyle.

Tanya Hackett

Table of Contents

Furthermore, the transmission, duplication, or reproduction of any of the following work including specific information will be considered an illegal act irrespective of if it is done electronically or in print. This extends to creating a secondary or tertiary copy of the work or a recorded copy and is only allowed with the express written consent from the Publisher. All additional right reserved.

The information in the following pages is broadly considered a truthful and accurate account of facts and as such, any inattention, use, or misuse of the information in question by the reader will render any resulting actions solely under their purview. There are no scenarios in which the publisher or the original author of this work can be in any fashion deemed liable for any hardship or damages that may befall them after undertaking information described herein.

Additionally, the information in the following pages is intended only for informational purposes and should thus be thought of as universal. As befitting its nature, it is presented without assurance regarding its prolonged validity or interim quality. Trademarks that are mentioned are done without written consent and can in no way be considered an endorsement from the trademark holder.

Introduction

An air fryer is a relatively new kitchen appliance that has proven to be very popular among consumers. While there are many different varieties available, most air fryers share many common features. They all have heating elements that circulate hot air to cook the food. Most come with pre-programmed settings that assist users in preparing a wide variety of foods. Air frying is a healthier style of cooking because it uses less oil than traditional deep frying methods. While it preserves the flavor and quality of the food, it reduces the amount of fat used in cooking. Air frying is a common method for "frying" foods that are primarily made with eggs and flour. These foods can be soft or crunchy to your preference by using this method.

How air fryers work

Air fryers use a blower to circulate hot air around food. The hot air heats the moisture on the food until it evaporates and creates steam. As steam builds up around the food, it creates pressure that pulls moisture from the surface of the food and pushes it away from the center, forming small bubbles. The bubbles creates a layer of air that surrounds the food and creates a crispy crust.

Choosing an air fryer

When choosing an air fryer, look for one that has good reviews for customer satisfaction. Start with the features you need, such as power, capacity size and accessories. Look for one that is easy to use. Some air fryers on the market have a built-in timer and adjustable temperature. Look for one with a funnel to catch grease, a basket that is dishwasher-safe and parts that are easy to clean.

How To Use An Air Fryer

For best results, preheat the air fryer at 400 F for 10 minutes. Preheating the air fryer allows it to reach the right temperature faster. In addition, preheating the air fryer is essential to ensure that your food won't burn.

How to cook stuff in an Air Fryer

If you don't have an air fryer yet, you can start playing with your ovens by throwing some frozen fries in there and cooking them until they are browned evenly. Depending on your oven, take a look at the temperature. You may need to increase or decrease the time.

What Foods Can You Cook In An Air Fryer?

Eggs: While you can cook eggs in an air fryer, we don't recommend it because you can't control the cooking time and temperature as precisely as with a traditional frying pan or skillet. It's much easier to get unevenly cooked eggs. You also can't toss in any sauces or seasonings and you won't get crispy, golden brown edges.

Frozen foods: Generally, frozen foods are best cooked in the conventional oven because they need to reach a certain temperature to be properly cooked. The air fryer is not capable of reaching temperatures that result in food being fully cooked.

Dehydrated Foods: Dehydrated foods require deep-frying, which is not something you can do with an air fryer. When it comes to cooking dehydrated foods, the air fryer is not the best option.

Vegetables: You can cook vegetables in an air fryer but you have to make sure that the air fryer is not set at a temperature that will burn them.

To ensure that your vegetables aren't overcooked, start the air fryer with the basket off, then toss in the veggies once the air has heated up and there are no more cold spots.

Make sure to stir the vegetables every few minutes. Cooking them in the basket is also an option, but they may stick together a little bit.

Fries: Frying fries in an air fryer is a good way to get crispy, golden-brown fries without adding lots of oil. Compared to conventional frying, air frying yields fewer calories.

To cook french fries in an air fryer, use a basket or a rack and pour in enough oil to come about halfway up the height of the fries. For best results, make sure the fries are frozen. Turn the air fryer onto 400 degrees and set it for 12 minutes. If you want them extra crispy, you can set it for 18 minutes, but they may burn a bit.

Benefits of an air fryer:

• It's one of the easiest ways to cook healthy foods. Used 4-5 times a week, it's a healthier option than frying with oil in your conventional oven or using canned foods.

• Air fryer meals are an easy way to serve tasty food that doesn't take up lots of space. Air fryers make it possible to cook three times as much food as you can in your microwave.

• Air fryers have a small footprint and you can store them away in a cabinet when not in use.

•They are versatile kitchen appliances. You can use them to cook food for lunch, dinner and snacks.

• Air fryers require little to no fussing in the kitchen. You can use them with the lid on, which means there's less washing up to do.

Honey Mustard Salmon

Preparation Time: 10 minutes

Cooking Time: 9 minutes

Servings: 2

Ingredients:

- 2 salmon fillets
- 2 tbsp Dijon mustard
- 2 tbsp honey
- 1/4 cup mayonnaise

- Salt and Pepper

Directions:

1. In a small dish, mix mustard, honey, mayonnaise, pepper, and salt together and brush over salmon.
2. Place the dehydrating tray in a multi-level air fryer basket and place basket in the air fryer.
3. Place salmon fillets on dehydrating tray.
4. Seal pot with air fryer lid and select air fry mode then set the temperature to 350 f and timer for 9 minutes.
5. Serve and enjoy.

Nutrition:

Calories 424

Fat 21.4 g

Carbohydrates 25.2 g

Sugar 19.3 g

Protein 35.5 g

Cholesterol 86 mg

Classic Tilapia

Preparation Time: 10 minutes

Cooking Time: 8 minutes

Servings: 2

Ingredients:

- 2 tilapia fillets
- 1 cup breadcrumbs
- 2 tbsp olive oil

Directions:

1. Brush fish fillets with oil then coat with breadcrumbs.
2. Place the dehydrating tray in a multi-level air fryer basket and place basket in the air fryer.
3. Place coated fish fillets on dehydrating tray.
4. Seal pot with air fryer lid and select air fry mode then set the temperature to 370 f and timer for 8 minutes.
5. Serve and enjoy.

Nutrition:

Calories 426

Fat 17.9 g

Carbohydrates 38.9 g

Sugar 3.4 g

Protein 28.2 g

Cholesterol 55 mg

Coconut Crusted Fish Fillets

Preparation Time: 10 minutes

Cooking Time: 8 minutes

Servings: 2

Ingredients:

- 2 tilapia fillets
- 1 egg, lightly beaten
- 1/4 cup coconut flour
- 1/2 cup flaked coconut
- Salt

Directions:

1. In a small dish, mix coconut flour, flaked coconut, and salt together.

2. Dip fish fillets in egg then coat with coconut flour mixture.
3. Place the dehydrating tray in a multi-level air fryer basket and place basket in the air fryer.
4. Place coated fish fillets on dehydrating tray.
5. Seal pot with air fryer lid and select air fry mode then set the temperature to 400 f and timer for 8 minutes. Turn fish fillets halfway through.
6. Serve and enjoy.

Nutrition:

Calories 255

Fat 11.4 g

Carbohydrates 13.2 g

Sugar 1.4 g

Protein 26.5 g

Cholesterol 137 mg

Tuna Patties

Preparation Time: 10 minutes

Cooking Time: 6 minutes

Servings: 4

Ingredients:

- 1 egg, lightly beaten
- 1/4 cup breadcrumbs
- 1 tbsp mustard
- Oz can tuna, drained
- Salt and Pepper

Directions:

1. Put all of the ingredients into the mixing bowl and mix until well combined.
2. Make four patties from mixture and place on a plate.
3. Place the dehydrating tray in a multi-level air fryer basket and place basket in the air fryer.
4. Place tuna patties on dehydrating tray.
5. Seal pot with air fryer lid and select air fry mode then set the temperature to 400 f and timer for 6 minutes. Turn patties halfway through.
6. Serve and enjoy.

Nutrition:

Calories 113

Fat 2.7 g

Carbohydrates 5.9 g

Sugar 0.7 g

Protein 15.6 g

Cholesterol 56 mg

Fish with Vegetables

Preparation Time: 10 minutes

Cooking Time: 25 minutes

Servings: 4

Ingredients:

- 1/2 lb. Cod fillet, cut into four pieces
- 1 cup cherry tomatoes
- 2 tbsp olive oil
- 1 cup baby potatoes, diced
- Salt and Pepper

Directions:

1. Line air fryer multi-level air fryer basket with aluminum foil.
2. Toss potatoes with half olive oil and add into the air fryer basket and place basket into the air fryer.
3. Seal pot with air fryer lid and select bake mode then set the temperature to 380 f and timer for 15 minutes.
4. Add cod and cherry tomatoes in the basket.
5. Drizzle with the excess oil and season with pepper and salt.
6. Seal pot with air fryer lid and select bake mode then set the temperature to 380 f and timer for 10 minutes.
7. Serve and enjoy.

Nutrition:

Calories 146

Fat 7.7 g

Carbohydrates 8.8 g

Sugar 1.2 g

Protein 12 g

Cholesterol 28 mg

Balsamic Salmon

Preparation Time: 10 minutes

Cooking Time: 3 minutes

Servings: 2

Ingredients:

- 2 salmon fillets
- 1 cup of water
- 2 tbsp balsamic vinegar
- 1 1/2 tbsp honey
- Salt and Pepper

Directions:

1. Season salmon with pepper and salt.
2. Mix together vinegar and honey.
3. Brush fish fillets with vinegar honey mixture.
4. Transfer water into the fryer then place trivet into the basket.
5. Place fish fillets on top of the trivet.
6. Seal fryer and cook on manual high pressure for 3 minutes.
7. As soon as the cooking is done, release pressure using the quick-release method then open the lid.

8. Garnish with parsley and serve.

Nutrition:

Calories 278

Fat 7.8 g

Carbohydrates 3.3 g

Sugar 0.5 g

Protein 46.8 g

Cholesterol 341 mg

Dijon Fish Fillets

Preparation Time: 10 minutes

Cooking Time: 3 minutes

Servings: 2

Ingredients:

- 2 halibut fillets
- 1 tbsp Dijon mustard
- 1 1/2 cups water
- Pepper
- Salt

Directions:

1. Transfer water into the air fryer then place steamer basket
2. Season fish fillets with pepper and salt and brush with Dijon mustard.
3. Place fish fillets in the steamer basket.
4. Seal fryer and cook on manual high pressure for 3 minutes.
5. After the cooking is done, release pressure using the quick-release method than open the lid.
6. Serve and enjoy.

Nutrition:

Calories 323

Fat 7 g

Carbohydrates 0.5 g

Sugar 0.1 g

Protein 60.9 g

Cholesterol 93 mg

Perfect Salmon Dinner

Preparation Time: 10 minutes

Cooking Time: 2 minutes

Servings: 3

Ingredients:

- 1 lb. Salmon fillet, cut into three pieces

- 2 garlic cloves, minced
- 1/2 tsp ground cumin
- 1 tsp red chili powder
- Salt and Pepper

Directions:

1. Discharge 1 1/2 cups water into the air fryer then place trivet into the pot.
2. In a small bowl, mix together garlic, cumin, chili powder, pepper, and salt.
3. Rub salmon with spice mixture and place on top of the trivet.
4. Seal pot with lid and cook on steam mode for 2 minutes.
5. After the cooking is done, release pressure using the quick-release method than open the lid.
6. Serve and enjoy.

Nutrition:

Calories 211

Fat 7 g

Carbohydrates 0.5 g

Sugar 0.1 g

Protein 60.9 g

Cholesterol 93 mg

Steam Clams

Preparation Time: 10 minutes

Cooking Time: 3 minutes

Servings: 3

Ingredients:

- 1 lb. Mushy shell clams
- 2 tbsp butter, melted
- 1/4 cup white wine
- 1/2 tsp garlic powder
- 1/4 cup fresh lemon juice

Directions:

1. Add white wine, lemon juice, garlic powder, and butter into the air fryer.
2. Place trivet into the pot.
3. Arrange clams on top of the trivet.
4. Seal pot and cook on manual high pressure for 3 minutes.
5. Once done then allow to release pressure naturally then open the lid.
6. Serve and enjoy.

Nutrition:

Calories 336

Fat 7 g

Carbohydrates 0.5 g

Sugar 0.1 g

Protein 60.9 g

Zucchini Curry

Preparation Time: 5 Minutes

Cooking Time: 8-10 Minutes

Ingredients:

1. 2Zucchinis, Washed & Sliced

2. 1 Tablespoon Olive Oil

3. Pinch Sea Salt

4. Curry Mix, Pre-Made

Directions:

- Turn on your air fryer to 390.

- Combine your zucchini slices, salt, oil, and spices.
- Put the zucchini into the air fryer, cooking for eight to ten minutes.
- You can serve alone or with sour cream.

Nutrition:

Calories: 100

Fat: 1

Carbs: 4

Protein: 2

Healthy Carrot Fries

Preparation Time: 5 Minutes

Cooking Time: 12-15 Minutes

Ingredients:

- 5Large Carrots
- 1 Tablespoon Olive Oil
- ½ Teaspoon Sea Salt

Directions:

1. Heat your air fryer to 390, and then wash and peel your carrots. Cut them in a way to form fries.
2. Combine your carrot sticks with your olive oil and salt, coating evenly.
3. Place them into the air fryer, cooking for twelve minutes. If they're not as crispy as you desire, then cook for two to three more minutes.
4. Serve with sour cream, ketchup or just with your favorite main dish.

Nutrition:

Calories: 140

Fat: 3

Carbs: 6

Protein: 7

Simple Stuffed Potatoes

Preparation Time: 15 Minutes

Cooking Time: 35 Minutes

Ingredients:

- 4Large Potatoes, Peeled
- 2Bacon, Rashers
- ½ Brown Onion, Diced
- ¼ Cup Cheese, Grated

Directions:

1. Start by heating your air fryer to 350.
2. Cut your potatoes in half, and then brush the potatoes with oil.
3. Put it in your air fryer, and cook for ten minutes. Brush the potatoes with oil again and bake for another ten minutes.
4. Make a whole in the baked potato to get them ready to stuff.
5. Sauté the bacon and onion in a frying pan. You should do this over medium heat, adding cheese and stir. Remove from heat.
6. Stuff your potatoes, and cook for four to five minutes.

Nutrition:

Calories: 180

Fat: 8

Carbs: 10

Protein: 11

Simple Roasted Carrots

Preparation Time: 5 Minutes

Cooking Time: 35 Minutes

Ingredients:

- 4Cups Carrots, Chopped
- 1 Teaspoon Herbs de Provence
- 2Teaspoons Olive Oil
- 4Tablespoons Orange Juice

Directions:

1. Start by preheating your air fryer to 320 degrees.
2. Combine your carrot pieces with your herbs and oil.
3. Cook for twenty-five to twenty-eight minutes.
4. Take it out and dip the pieces in orange juice before frying for an additional seven minutes.

Nutrition:

Calories: 125

Fat: 2

Carbs: 5

Protein: 6

Broccoli & Cheese

Preparation Time: 5 Minutes

Cooking Time: 9 Minutes

Ingredients:

- 1 Head Broccoli, Washed & Chopped
- Salt & Pepper to Taste
- 1 Tablespoon Olive oil
- Sharp Cheddar Cheese, Shredded

Directions:

1. Start by putting your air fryer to 360.
2. Combine your broccoli with your olive oil and sea salt.
3. Place it in the air fryer, and cook for six minutes.
4. Take it out, and then top with cheese, cooking for another three minutes.
5. Serve with your choice of protein.

Nutrition:

Calories: 170

Fat: 5

Carbs: 9

Protein: 7

Fried Plantains

Preparation Time: 5 minutes

Cooking Time: 10 minutes

Servings: 2

Ingredients:

- 2ripe plantains, peeled and cut at a diagonal into ½-inch-thick pieces
- 3tablespoons ghee, melted
- ¼ teaspoon kosher salt

Directions

1. Preparing the Ingredients. In a bowl, mix the plantains with the ghee and salt.
2. Air Frying. Arrange the plantain pieces in the air fryer basket. Set the air fryer to 400°F for 8 minutes. The plantains are done when they are soft and tender on the inside, and have plenty of crisp, sweet, brown spots on the outside.

Nutrition:

Calories: 180

Fat: 5

Carbs: 10

Protein: 7

Bacon-Wrapped Asparagus

Preparation Time: 5 minutes

Cooking Time: 10 minutes

Servings: 4

Ingredients:

- 1 pound asparagus, trimmed (about 24 spears)
- 4slices bacon or beef bacon
- ½ cup Ranch Dressin for serving
- 3tablespoons chopped fresh chives, for garnish

Directions

1. Preparing the Ingredients. Grease the air fryer basket with avocado oil. Preheat the air fryer to 400°F.

2. Slice the bacon down the middle, making long, thin strips. Wrap 1 slice of bacon around 3 asparagus spears and secure each end with a toothpick. Repeat with the remaining bacon and asparagus.

3. Air Frying. Place the asparagus bundles in the air fryer in a single layer. (If you're using a smaller air fryer, cook in batches if necessary.) Cook for 8 minutes for thin stalks, 10 minutes for medium to thick stalks, or until the asparagus is slightly charred on the ends and the bacon is crispy.
4. Serve with ranch dressing and garnish with chives. Best served fresh.

Nutrition:

Calories 241;

Fat 22g;

Protein 7g;

Total carbs 6g;

Fiber 3g

Air Fried Roasted Corn on The Cob

Preparation Time: 5 minutes

Cooking Time: 10 minutes

Servings: 4

Ingredients:

- 1 tablespoon vegetable oil
- 4ears of corn
- Unsalted butter, for topping
- Salt, for topping
- Freshly ground black pepper, for topping

Directions:

1. Preparing the Ingredients. Rub the vegetable oil onto the corn, coating it thoroughly.
2. Air Frying. Set the temperature of your AF to 400°F. Set the timer and grill for 5 minutes.
3. Using tongs, flip or rotate the corn.
4. Reset the timer and grill for 5 minutes more.
5. Serve with a pat of butter and a generous sprinkle of salt and pepper.

Nutrition:

Calories: 265;

Fat: 17g;

Carbohydrate: 29g;

Fiber: 4g;

Sugar: 5g;

Protein: 5g;

Green Beans & Bacon

Preparation Time: 15 minutes

Cooking Time: 20 minutes

Servings: 4

Ingredients:

- 3cups frozen cut green beans
- 1 medium onion, chopped
- 3slices bacon, chopped
- ¼ cup water
- Kosher salt and black pepper

Directions:

1. Preparing the Ingredients
2. In a 6 × 3-inch round heatproof pan, combine the frozen green beans, onion, bacon, and water. Toss to combine. Place the saucepan in the basket.
3. Air Frying
4. Set the air fryer to 375°F for 15 minutes.
5. Raise the air fryer temperature to 400°F for 5 minutes. Season the beans with salt and pepper to taste and toss well.

6. Remove the pan from the air fryer basket and cover with foil. Let it rest for 5 minutes then serve.

Nutrition:

Calories: 230

Fat: 10

Carbs: 14

Protein: 17

Air Fried Honey Roasted Carrots

Preparation Time: 5 minutes

Cooking Time: 15 minutes

Servings: 4

Ingredients:

- 3cups baby carrots
- 1 tablespoon extra-virgin olive oil
- 1 tablespoon honey

- Salt
- Freshly ground black pepper
- Fresh dill (optional)

Directions:

1. Preparing the Ingredients. In a bowl, combine honey, olive oil, carrots, salt, and pepper. Make sure that the carrots are thoroughly coated with oil. Place the carrots in the air fryer basket.
2. Air Frying. Set the temperature of your AF to 390°F. Set the timer and roast for 12 minutes, or until fork-tender.
3. Remove the air fryer drawer and release the air fryer basket. Pour the carrots into a bowl, sprinkle with dill, if desired, and serve.

Nutrition:

Calories: 140

Fat: 3

Carbs: 7

Protein: 9

Air Fried Roasted Cabbage

Preparation Time: 5 minutes

Cooking Time: 10 minutes

Servings: 4

Ingredients:

- 1 head cabbage, sliced in 1-inch-thick ribbons
- 1 tablespoon olive oil
- salt and freshly ground black pepper
- 1 teaspoon garlic powder
- 1 teaspoon red pepper flakes

Directions

1. Preparing the Ingredients. In a bowl, combine the olive oil, cabbage, salt, pepper, garlic powder, and red pepper flakes. Make sure that the cabbage is thoroughly coated with oil. Place the cabbage in the air fryer basket.

2. Air Frying. Set the temperature of your Air Fryer to 350°F. Set the timer and roast for 4 minutes.

3. Using tongs, flip the cabbage. Reset the timer and roast for 3 minutes more.

Nutrition:

Calories: 100

Fat: 1

Carbs: 3

Protein: 3

Burrata-Stuffed Tomatoes

Preparation Time: 5 minutes

Cooking Time: 5 minutes

Servings: 4

Ingredients:

- 4medium tomatoes
- ½ teaspoon fine sea salt
- 4(2-ounce) Burrata balls
- Fresh basil leaves, for garnish
- Extra-virgin olive oil, for drizzling

Directions

1. Preparing the Ingredients. Preheat the air fryer to 300°F.
2. Scoop out the tomato seeds and membranes using a melon baller or spoon. Sprinkle the insides of the tomatoes with the salt. Stuff each tomato with a ball of Burrata.
3. Air Frying. Put it in the fryer and cook for 5 minutes, or until the cheese has softened.
4. Garnish with olive oil and basil leaves. Serve warm.

Nutrition:

Calories 108;

Fat 7g;

Protein 6g;

Total Carbs 5g;

Fiber 2g

Broccoli with Parmesan Cheese

Preparation Time: 5 minutes

Cooking Time: 5 minutes

Servings: 4

Ingredients:

- 1pound broccoli florets
- 2teaspoons minced garlic
- 2tablespoons olive oil
- ¼ cup grated or shaved Parmesan cheese

Directions

1. Preparing the Ingredients. Preheat the air fryer to 360°F. In a bowl, mix together the broccoli florets, garlic, olive oil, and Parmesan cheese.
2. Air Frying. Place the broccoli in the air fryer basket in a single layer and set the timer and steam for 4 minutes.

Nutrition:

Calories: 130

Fat: 3

Carbs: 5

Protein: 4

Caramelized Broccoli

Preparation Time: 5 minutes

Cooking Time: 10 minutes

Servings: 4

Ingredients:

- 4cups broccoli florets
- 3tablespoons melted ghee or butter-flavored coconut oil
- 1½ teaspoons fine sea salt or smoked salt
- Mayonnaise, for serving (optional; omit for egg-free)

Directions

1. Preparing the Ingredients. Grease the basket with avocado oil. Preheat the air fryer to 400°F. Place the broccoli in a large bowl. Drizzle it with the ghee, toss to coat, and sprinkle it with the salt.
2. Air Frying. Transfer the broccoli to the air fryer basket and cook for 8 minutes, or until tender and crisp on the edges.

Nutrition:

Calories: 120

Fat: 2

Carbs: 4

Protein: 3

Brussels Sprouts with Balsamic Oil

Preparation Time: 5 minutes

Cooking Time: 15 minutes

Servings: 4

Ingredients:

- ¼ teaspoon salt
- 1 tablespoon balsamic vinegar
- 2cups Brussels sprouts, halved
- 3tablespoons olive oil

Directions:

1. Preparing the Ingredients. Preheat the air fryer for 5 minutes. Mix all ingredients in a bowl until the zucchini fries are well coated.
2. Air Frying. Place in the air fryer basket. Close and cook for 15 minutes for 350°F.

Nutrition:

Calories: 82;

Fat: 6.8g;

Protein: 1.5g

Spiced Butternut Squash

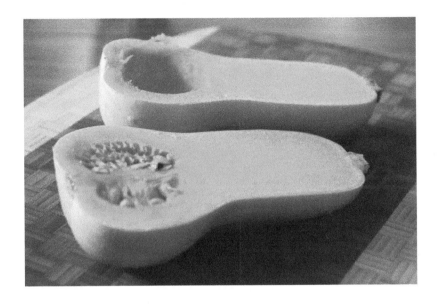

Preparation Time: 10 minutes

Cooking Time: 15 minutes

Servings: 4

Ingredients:

- 4cups 1-inch-cubed butternut squash
- 2tablespoons vegetable oil
- 1 to 2 tablespoons brown sugar
- 1 teaspoon Chinese five-spice powder

Directions

1. Preparing the Ingredients. In a bowl, combine the oil, sugar, squash, and five-spice powder. Toss to coat.
2. Place the squash in the air fryer basket.
3. Air Frying. Set the air fryer to 400°F for 15 minutes or until tender.

Nutrition:

Calories: 160

Fat: 5

Carbs: 9

Protein: 6

Garlic Thyme Mushrooms

Preparation Time: 5 minutes

Cooking Time: 10 minutes

Servings: 4

Ingredients:

- 3tablespoons unsalted butter, melted
- 1 (8-ounce) package button mushrooms, sliced
- 2cloves garlic, minced
- 3sprigs fresh thyme leaves
- ½ teaspoon fine sea salt

Directions:

1. Preparing the Ingredients. Grease the basket with avocado oil. Preheat the air fryer to 400°F.
2. Place all the ingredients in a medium-sized bowl. Use a spoon or your hands to coat the mushroom slices.
3. Air Frying. Put the mushrooms in the basket in one layer; work in batches if necessary. Cook for 10 minutes, or until slightly crispy and brown. Garnish with thyme sprigs before serving.
4. Reheat in a warmed up 350°F air fryer for 5 minutes, or until heated through.

Nutrition:

Calories 82;

Fat 9g;

Protein 1g;

Total carbs 1g;

Fiber 0.2g

Zucchini Parmesan Chips

Preparation Time: 10 minutes

Cooking Time: 10 minutes

Servings: 10

Ingredients:

- ½ tsp. paprika
- ½ C. grated parmesan cheese
- ½ C. Italian breadcrumbs
- 1 lightly beaten egg
- 2thinly sliced zucchinis

Directions:

1. Preparing the Ingredients. Use a very sharp knife or mandolin slicer to slice zucchini as thinly as you can. Pat off extra moisture. Beat egg with a pinch of pepper and salt and a bit of water.

2. Combine paprika, cheese, and breadcrumbs in a bowl. Dip slices of zucchini into the egg mixture and then into breadcrumb mixture. Press gently to coat.

3. Air Frying. With olive oil cooking spray, mist coated zucchini slices. Place into your Air fryer in a single layer. Set temperature to 350°F, and set time to 8 minutes. Sprinkle with salt and serve with salsa.

Nutrition:

Calories: 130

Fat: 2

Carbs: 5

Protein: 3

Jicama Fries

Preparation Time: 10 minutes

Cooking Time: 5 minutes

Servings: 4

Ingredients:

- 1 tbsp. dried thyme
- ¾ C. arrowroot flour
- ½ large Jicama
- Eggs

Directions:

1. Preparing the Ingredients. Sliced jicama into fries.
2. Whisk eggs together and pour over fries. Toss to coat.
3. Mix a pinch of salt, thyme, and arrowroot flour together. Toss egg-coated jicama into dry mixture, tossing to coat well.
4. Air Frying. Spray the air fryer basket with olive oil and add fries. Set temperature to 350°F, and set time to 5 minutes. Toss halfway into the cooking process.

Nutrition:

Calories: 211;

Fat: 19g;

Carbs: 16g;

Protein:9g

Cauliflower pizza crust

Preparation Time: 5 minutes

Cooking Time: 20 minutes

Servings: 6

Ingredients:

- 1(12-oz.) Steamer bag cauliflower
- 1 large egg.
- ½ cup shredded sharp cheddar cheese.
- 2tbsp. Blanched finely ground almond flour
- 1 tsp. Italian blend seasoning

Directions:

1. Cook cauliflower according to package. Take out from bag and place into a paper towel to remove excess water. Place cauliflower into a large bowl.

2. Add almond flour, cheese, egg, and italian seasoning to the bowl and mix well

3. Cut a piece of parchment to fit your air fryer basket. Press cauliflower into 6-inch round circle. Place into the air fryer basket. Adjust the temperature to 360 degrees f and set the timer for 11 minutes. After 7 minutes, flip the pizza crust

4. Add preferred toppings to pizza. Place back into air fryer basket and cook an additional 4 minutes or until fully cooked and golden. Serve immediately.

Nutrition:

Calories: 230;

Protein: 14.9g;

Fiber: 4.7g;

Fat: 14.2g;

Carbs: 10.0g

Savoy cabbage and tomatoes

Preparation Time: 5 minutes

Cooking Time: 20 minutes

Servings: 4

Ingredients:

- 2spring onions; chopped.

- 1 savoy cabbage, shredded

- 1 tbsp. Parsley; chopped.

- 2tbsp. Tomato sauce

- Salt and black pepper to taste.

Directions:

1. In a pan that fits your air fryer, mix the cabbage the rest of the ingredients except the parsley, toss, put the pan in the fryer and cook at 360°f for 15 minutes

2. Divide between plates and serve with parsley sprinkled on top.

Nutrition:

Calories: 163;

Fat: 4g;

Fiber: 3g;

Carbs: 6g;

Protein: 7g

Cauliflower steak

Preparation Time: 5 minutes

Cooking Time: 10 minutes

Servings: 4

Ingredients:

- 1 medium head cauliflower
- ¼ cup blue cheese crumbles
- ¼ cup hot sauce
- ¼ cup full-fat ranch dressing
- 2tbsp. Salted butter; melted.

Directions:

1. Remove cauliflower leaves. Slice the head in ½-inch-thick slices.
2. In a small bowl, mix hot sauce and butter. Brush the mixture over the cauliflower.
3. Place each cauliflower steak into the air fryer, working in batches if necessary. Adjust the temperature to 400 degrees f and set the timer for 7 minutes

4. When cooked, edges will begin turning dark and caramelized. To serve, sprinkle steaks with crumbled blue cheese. Drizzle with ranch dressing.

Nutrition:

Calories: 122;

Protein: 4.9g;

Fiber: 3.0g;

Fat: 8.4g;

Carbs: 7.7g

Tomato, avocado and green beans

Preparation Time: 5 minutes

Cooking Time: 20 minutes

Servings: 4

Ingredients:

- ¼ lb. Green beans, trimmed and halved
- 1 avocado, peeled, pitted and cubed
- 1 pint mixed cherry tomatoes; halved
- 2tbsp. Olive oil

Directions:

1. In a pan that fits your air fryer, mix the tomatoes with the rest of the ingredients, toss.
2. Put the pan in the fryer and cook at 360°f for 15 minutes. Transfer to bowls and serve

Nutrition:

Calories: 151;

Fat: 3g;

Fiber: 2g;

Carbs: 4g;

Protein: 4g

Dill and garlic green beans

Preparation Time: 5 minutes

Cooking Time: 20 minutes

Servings: 4

Ingredients:

- 1 lb. Green beans, trimmed
- ½ cup bacon, cooked and chopped.
- 2garlic cloves; minced

- 2tbsp. Dill; chopped.
- Salt and black pepper to taste.

Directions:

1. In a pan that fits the air fryer, combine the green beans with the rest of the ingredients, toss.
2. Put the pan in the fryer and cook at 390°f for 15 minutes
3. Divide everything between plates and serve.

Nutrition:

Calories: 180;

Fat: 3g;

Fiber: 2g;

Carbs: 4g;

Protein: 6g

Eggplant stacks

Preparation Time: 5 minutes

Cooking Time: 15 minutes

Servings: 4

Ingredients:

- 2large tomatoes; cut into ¼-inch slices
- ¼ cup fresh basil, sliced
- 4oz. Fresh mozzarella; cut into ½-oz. Slices
- 1 medium eggplant; cut into ¼-inch slices
- 2tbsp. Olive oil

Directions:

1. In a 6-inch round baking dish, place four slices of eggplant on the bottom. Put a slice of tomato on each eggplant round, then mozzarella, then eggplant. Repeat as necessary.

2. Drizzle with olive oil. Cover dish with foil and place dish into the air fryer basket. Adjust the temperature to 350 degrees f and set the timer for 12 minutes.

3. When done, eggplant will be tender. Garnish with fresh basil to serve.

Nutrition:

Calories: 195;

Protein: 8.5g;

Fiber: 5.2g;

Fat: 12.7g;

Carbs: 12.7g

Air Fried Spaghetti Squash

Preparation Time: 5 minutes

Cooking Time: 50 minutes

Servings: 4

Ingredients:

- ½ large spaghetti squash
- 2tbsp. Salted butter; melted.
- 1 tbsp. Coconut oil
- 1tsp. Dried parsley.
- ½tsp. Garlic powder.

Directions:

1. Brush shell of spaghetti squash with coconut oil. Place the skin side down and brush the inside with butter. Sprinkle with garlic powder and parsley.
2. Place squash with the skin side down into the air fryer basket. Adjust the temperature to 350 degrees f and set the timer for 30 minutes
3. When the timer beeps, flip the squash so skin side is up and cook an additional 15 minutes or until fork tender. Serve warm.

Nutrition:

Calories: 182;

Protein: 1.9g;

Fiber: 3.9g;

Fat: 11.7g;

Carbs: 18.2g

Beets and Blue Cheese Salad

Preparation Time: 10 minutes

Cooking Time: 15 minutes

Servings: 6

Ingredients:

- 6beets, peeled and quartered
- Salt and black pepper to the taste
- ¼ cup blue cheese, crumbled
- 1 tablespoon olive oil

Directions:

1. Put beets in your air fryer, cook them at 350 degrees F for 14 minutes and transfer them to a bowl. Add blue cheese, salt, pepper and oil, toss and serve. Enjoy!

Nutrition:

Calories 100,

Fat 4,

Fiber 4,

Carbs 10,

Protein 5

Broccoli Salad

Preparation Time: 10 minutes

Cooking Time: 10 minutes

Servings: 4

Ingredients:

- 1 broccoli head, with separated florets
- 1 tbsp. peanut oil
- 6cloves of garlic, minced
- 1 tbsp. Chinese rice wine vinegar
- Salt and black pepper to taste

Directions:

1. In a bowl, mix broccoli half of the oil with salt, pepper and, toss, transfer to your air fryer and cook at 350 degrees F for 8 minutes. Halfway through, shake the fryer. Take the broccoli out and put it into a salad bowl, add the rest of the peanut oil, garlic and rice vinegar, mix really well and serve. Enjoy!

Nutrition:

Calories 121,

Fat 3,

Fiber 4,

Carbs 4,

Protein 4

Roasted Brussels Sprouts with Tomatoes

Preparation Time: 5 minutes

Cooking Time: 10 minutes

Servings: 4

Ingredients:

- 1-pound Brussels sprouts, trimmed
- Salt and black pepper to the taste
- 6cherry tomatoes, halved
- ¼ cup green onions, chopped
- 1 tablespoon olive oil

Directions:

1. Season Brussels sprouts with salt and pepper, put them in your air fryer and cook at 350 degrees F for 10 minutes. Transfer them to a bowl, add salt, pepper, cherry tomatoes, green onions and olive oil, toss well and serve. Enjoy!

Nutrition:

Calories 121,

Fat 4,

Fiber 4,

Carbs 11,

Protein 4

Cheesy Brussels Sprouts

Preparation Time: 10 minutes

Cooking Time: 10 minutes

Servings: 4

Ingredients:

- 1-pound Brussels sprouts, washed
- Juice of 1 lemon
- Salt and black pepper to the taste
- 2tablespoons butter
- 3tablespoons parmesan, grated

Directions:

1. Put Brussels sprouts in your air fryer, cook them at 350 degrees F for 8 minutes and transfer them to a bowl. Warm up a pan over moderate heat with the butter, then add lemon juice, salt and pepper, whisk well and add to Brussels sprouts. Add parmesan, toss until parmesan melts and serve. Enjoy!

Nutrition:

Calories 152,

Fat 6,

Fiber 6,

Carbs 8,

Protein 12

Sweet Baby Carrots Dish

Preparation Time: 10 minutes

Cooking Time: 10 minutes

Servings: 4

Ingredients:

- 2cups baby carrots
- A pinch of salt and black pepper
- 1 tablespoon brown sugar
- ½ tablespoon butter, melted

Directions:

1. In a dish that fits your air fryer, mix baby carrots with butter, salt, pepper and sugar, toss, introduce in your air fryer and cook at 350 degrees F for 10 minutes. Divide among plates and serve. Enjoy!

Nutrition:

Calories 100,

Fat 2,

Fiber 3,

Carbs 7,

Protein 4

Seasoned Leeks

Preparation Time: 10 minutes

Cooking Time: 10 minutes

Servings: 4

Ingredients:

- 4leeks, washed, halved
- Salt and black pepper to taste
- 1 tbsp. butter, melted
- 1 tbsp. lemon juice

Directions:

1. Rub leeks with melted butter, season with salt and pepper, put in your air fryer and cook at 350 degrees F for 7 minutes. Arrange on a platter, drizzle lemon juice all over and serve. Enjoy!

Nutrition:

Calories 100,

Fat 4,

Fiber 2,

Carbs 6,

Protein 2

Crispy Potatoes and Parsley

Preparation Time: 10 minutes

Cooking Time: 10 minutes

Servings: 4

Ingredients:

- 1-pound gold potatoes, cut into wedges
- Salt and black pepper to the taste
- 2tablespoons olive
- Juice from ½ lemon
- ¼ cup parsley leaves, chopped

Directions:

1. Rub potatoes with salt, pepper, lemon juice and olive oil, put them in your air fryer and cook at 350 degrees F for 10 minutes. Divide among plates, sprinkle parsley on top and serve. Enjoy!

Nutrition:

Calories 152,

Fat 3,

Fiber 7,

Carbs 17,

Protein 4

Garlic Tomatoes

Preparation Time: 10 minutes

Cooking Time: 15 minutes

Servings: 4

Ingredients:

- 4garlic cloves, crushed
- 1-pound mixed cherry tomatoes
- 3thyme springs, chopped
- Salt and black pepper to the taste
- ¼ cup olive oil

Directions:

1. In a bowl, mix tomatoes with salt, black pepper, garlic, olive oil and thyme, toss to coat, introduce in your air fryer and cook at 360 degrees F for 15 minutes. Divide tomatoes mix on plates and serve. Enjoy!

Nutrition:

Calories 100,

Fat 0,

Fiber 1,

Carbs 1,

Protein 6

Easy Green Beans and Potatoes

Preparation Time: 10 minutes

Cooking Time: 15 minutes

Servings: 5

Ingredients:

- 2pounds green beans
- 6new potatoes, halved
- Salt and black pepper to the taste
- A drizzle of olive oil
- 6bacon slices, cooked and chopped

Directions:

1. In a bowl, mix green beans with potatoes, salt, pepper and oil, toss, transfer to your air fryer and cook at 390 degrees F for 15 minutes. Divide among plates and serve with bacon sprinkled on top. Enjoy!

Nutrition:

Calories 374,

Fat 15,

Fiber 12,

Carbs 28,

Protein 12

Green Beans and Tomatoes

Preparation Time: 10 minutes

Cooking Time: 15 minutes

Servings: 4

Ingredients:

- 1 pint cherry tomatoes
- 1 pound green beans
- 2tablespoons olive oil
- Salt and black pepper to the taste

Directions:

1. In a bowl, mix cherry tomatoes with green beans, olive oil, salt and pepper, toss, transfer to your air fryer and cook at 400 degrees F for 15 minutes. Divide among plates and serve right away. Enjoy!

Nutrition:

Calories 162,

Fat 6,

Fiber 5,

Carbs 8,

Protein 9

Flavoured Asparagus

Preparation Time: 5 minutes

Cooking Time: 30 minutes

Servings: 2

Ingredients:

- Nutritional yeast
- Olive oil non-stick spray
- One bunch of asparagus

Directions:

1. Wash asparagus and then cut off the bushy, woody ends.

2. Drizzle asparagus with olive oil spray and sprinkle with yeast. In your air fryer, lay asparagus in a singular layer. Cook 8 minutes at 360 degrees.

Nutrition:

Calories: 17 Cal

Fat: 4 g

Carbs: 32 g

Protein: 24 g

Avocado Fries

Preparation Time: 5 minutes

Cooking Time: 5 minutes

Servings: 6

Ingredients:

- 1 avocado
- ½ tsp. salt
- ½ C. panko breadcrumbs
- Bean liquid (aquafaba) from a 15-ounce can of white or garbanzo beans

Directions:

1. Peel, pit, and slice up avocado. Toss salt and breadcrumbs together in a bowl. Place aquafaba into another bowl. Dredge slices of avocado first in aquafaba and then in panko, making sure you get an even coating. Place coated avocado slices into a single layer in the air fryer. Cook 5 minutes at 390 degrees, shaking at 5 minutes. Serve with your favorite keto dipping sauce!

Nutrition:

Calories: 102

Fat: 22g

Protein: 9g

Sugar: 1g

Spaghetti Squash Tots

Preparation Time: 5 minutes

Cooking Time: 15 minutes

Servings: 10

Ingredients:

- ¼ tsp. pepper
- ½ tsp. salt
- 1 thinly sliced scallion
- 1 spaghetti squash

Directions:

1. Wash and cut the squash in lengthwise. Scrape out the seeds. With a fork, remove spaghetti meat by strands and throw out skins. In a clean towel, toss in squash and wring out as much moisture as possible. Place in a bowl and with a knife slice through meat a few times to cut up smaller. Add pepper, salt, and scallions to squash and mix well. Create "tot" shapes with your hands and place in air fryer. Spray with olive oil. Cook 15 minutes at 350 degrees until golden and crispy!

Nutrition:

Calories: 231

Fat: 18g

Protein: 5g

Sugar: 0g

Cinnamon Butternut Squash Fries

Preparation Time: 10 minutes

Cooking Time: 10 minutes

Servings: 2

Ingredients:

- 1 pinch of salt
- 1 tbsp. powdered unprocessed sugar
- 2tsp. cinnamon
- 1 tbsp. coconut oil
- 10ounces pre-cut butternut squash fries

Directions:

1. In a plastic bag, pour in all ingredients. Coat fries with other components till coated and sugar is dissolved. Spread coated fries into a single layer in the air fryer. Cook 10 minutes at 390 degrees until crispy.

Nutrition:

Calories: 175

Fat: 8g

Protein: 1g

Sugar: 5g

Lemon bell peppers

Preparation Time: 20 minutes

Cooking Time: 15 minutes

Servings: 4

Ingredients:

- 1 ½ lb. Mixed bell peppers; halved and deseeded
- 2tbsp. Lemon juice
- 2tbsp. Balsamic vinegar
- 2tsp. Lemon zest, grated
- A handful parsley; chopped.

Directions:

1. Put the peppers in your air fryer's basket and cook at 350°f for 15 minutes. Peel the bell peppers, mix them with the rest of the ingredients, toss and serve

Nutrition:

Calories: 151;

Fat: 2g;

Fiber: 3g;

Carbs: 5g;

Protein: 5g

30-Day Meal Plan

Day	Breakfast	Lunch/dinner	Dessert
1	Shrimp Skillet	Spinach Rolls	Matcha Crepe Cake
2	Coconut Yogurt with Chia Seeds	Goat Cheese Fold-Overs	Pumpkin Spices Mini Pies
3	Chia Pudding	Crepe Pie	Nut Bars
4	Egg Fat Bombs	Coconut Soup	Pound Cake
5	Morning "Grits"	Fish Tacos	Tortilla Chips with Cinnamon Recipe
6	Scotch Eggs	Cobb Salad	Granola Yogurt with Berries
7	Bacon Sandwich	Cheese Soup	Berry Sorbet

8	Noatmeal	Tuna Tartare	Coconut Berry Smoothie
9	Breakfast Bake with Meat	Clam Chowder	Coconut Milk Banana Smoothie
10	Breakfast Bagel	Asian Beef Salad	Mango Pineapple Smoothie
11	Egg and Vegetable Hash	Keto Carbonara	Raspberry Green Smoothie
12	Cowboy Skillet	Cauliflower Soup with Seeds	Loaded Berries Smoothie
13	Feta Quiche	Prosciutto-Wrapped Asparagus	Papaya Banana and Kale Smoothie
14	Bacon Pancakes	Stuffed Bell Peppers	Green Orange Smoothie

15	Waffles	Stuffed Eggplants with Goat Cheese	Double Berries Smoothie
16	Chocolate Shake	Korma Curry	Energizing Protein Bars
17	Eggs in Portobello Mushroom Hats	Zucchini Bars	Sweet and Nutty Brownies
18	Matcha Fat Bombs	Mushroom Soup	Keto Macho Nachos
19	Keto Smoothie Bowl	Stuffed Portobello Mushrooms	Peanut Butter Choco Banana Gelato with Mint
20	Salmon Omelet	Lettuce Salad	Cinnamon Peaches and Yogurt
21	Hash Brown	Onion Soup	Pear Mint Honey Popsicles

22	Black's Bangin' Casserole	Asparagus Salad	Orange and Peaches Smoothie
23	Bacon Cups	Cauliflower Tabbouleh	Coconut Spiced Apple Smoothie
24	Spinach Eggs and Cheese	Beef Salpicao	Sweet and Nutty Smoothie
25	Taco Wraps	Stuffed Artichoke	Ginger Berry Smoothie
26	Coffee Donuts	Spinach Rolls	Vegetarian Friendly Smoothie
27	Egg Baked Omelet	Goat Cheese Fold-Overs	ChocNut Smoothie
28	Ranch Risotto	Crepe Pie	Coco Strawberry Smoothie
29	Scotch Eggs	Coconut Soup	Egg Spinach Berries Smoothie

30	Fried Eggs	Fish Tacos	Creamy Dessert Smoothie

Conclusion

Thanks for making it to the end of this book. An air fryer is a relatively new addition to the kitchen, and it's easy to see why people are getting excited about using it. With an air fryer, you can make crispy fries, chicken wings, chicken breasts and steaks in minutes. There are many delicious foods that you can prepare without adding oil or grease to your meal. Again make sure to read the instructions on your air fryer and follow the rules for proper usage and maintenance. Once your air fryer is in good working condition, you can really get creative and start experimenting your way to healthy food that tastes great.

That's it! Thank you!

CPSIA information can be obtained
at www.ICGtesting.com
Printed in the USA
BVHW091055220221
600778BV00007B/782

9 781801 750424